How To Do Well And Boost Your Confidence At Work
By Jean Young

EXPERIENCE EVERYTHING
P U B L I S H I N G

Disclaimer

This document is geared towards providing exact and reliable information in regards to the topic and issue covered. The publication is sold with the idea that the publisher is not required to render accounting, officially permitted, or otherwise, qualified services. If advice is necessary, legal or professional, a practiced individual in the profession should be ordered.

- From a Declaration of Principles which was accepted and approved equally by a Committee of the American Bar Association and a Committee of Publishers and Associations:

The information herein is offered for informational purposes solely, and is universal as so. The presentation of the information is without contract or any type of guarantee assurance.

Introduction

Does your confidence level affect your performance at work?

Section 1: Boosting Your Confidence At Work

Section 2: How To Excel At Work

Conclusion

Introduction

Why do you need to excel at work?

First of all, employers want employees that have very strong ethics when it comes to work. Employers prefer to have employees that will do their best at work and deliver projects and tasks on time. These are the kind of employees that employers would not hesitate to promote. They know that employees who excel can be depended on. When you have a strong work ethic, you are opening the doors for opportunities and you are also building a reputation for yourself.

Second, your performance greatly depends on it. Any company would rather have a person that has the skills and the drive to excel at work. When you are capable of excelling at work, you can also get references from that job and this will make you more desirable for the companies that you are applying for.

When somebody recognizes and appreciates the effort that you have done, it makes you feel good. You get a sense of satisfaction knowing that you are doing things well. The same thing is applicable when you excel at work. You are satisfied with the work that you are doing because you know your employers see your value and they know that the job that you are doing is necessary for the whole operation to succeed.

When you strive to excel in your work, you will see your career grow as a result. Your employer will surely see the effort that you are putting in your work and they like employees with that kind of drive. As mentioned earlier, these are the kinds of employees that they want to promote. And so, having a strong work ethic and excelling at work will help you achieve higher positions in your career.

Why do you need to be confident?

Being truly confident has many benefits that can greatly impact your work, relationships and pretty much everything that you do in life. Below are some reasons why you should be more confident regardless of where you are.

1 When you are confident, you can get more things done. It is not in you to procrastinate. You do not make excuses when it comes to the things that you have to do. You just do what you have to do because you know it is the right thing. You know that whatever you are doing right now, it will pay off.

2 You do not worry about unnecessary things when you are confident. You trust yourself enough. You know that whatever is going to happen, you will be able to pull through.

3 A lot of people find truly confident people to be sexier than those barely wearing anything or those people with perfect bodies. Even companies recruiting new employers find potential employees that exude confidence to be more attractive than those who do not believe in themselves. You think your lack of confidence will not show but people are good at picking up signs of it. They can easily tell a confident person apart from one who does not have any confidence at all.

4 You do not worry about how people look at you or if they are going to judge you. You can just be yourself and it is easier for you to connect with others and build new relationships.

5 Because you won't be spending much time worrying about unnecessary things, you can concentrate on the brighter side of things. This means that a person that is confident is likely to have more fun and enjoy the lighter side of life.

6   Many people hesitate to take a step forward because they fear they might not be good enough or they think they cannot do it. But this is not going to be a problem for people who are confident. A confident person knows exactly what they can and cannot do and will not hesitate to take any opportunity that comes his way. His confidence acts like his security blanket. Despite fearing something, they will still move forward because they knows that they can do it.

7   Confident people know when to prioritize themselves. They don't fear that their boss will think less of them for taking some time for themselves such as going on vacation. And when you're well rested, you are going to do better at work anyway.

8   There are times that people do not speak up even though they know they are right. This is due to their lack of confidence. But a person that has confidence will not be afraid to speak up and be heard.

9   Expanding your connection is not going to be a problem if you are confident. Meeting new people is much easier for you and you do not worry about being judged or if they don't like you.

Does your confidence level affect your performance at work?

The level of confidence that you have has a great impact on how well you will be able to perform at work. Imagine this scenario: your boss has just presented an idea that they think would do well on your next ad campaign. However, you see something in thier presentation that is not quite right. But because you are afraid your opinion might get rejected or you are afraid that your boss would get afraid of you, you decide not to say anything about it.

When you are not confident enough, you never have the guts to speak up and be heard no matter how right your opinion is. You prefer to just keep your head down and obey what others say. This can result in many things. Your colleagues might take advantage of this knowing that you won't be complaining. When you are not confident enough, you do not have enough guts to grab opportunities that you know you deserve. You just say yes to whatever your boss says because you do not want to argue.

Lack of confidence will also affect how you perform at work. When you are required to make decisions, you find it hard to make one without having others confirm or back your decision. It is easy to find yourself being dependent on others. And you are constantly seeking for the approval of others. A person who lacks confidence is not as appealing to employers when it comes to which employees should be promoted.

So as you can see, one of the things that you need to do in order for you to succeed and excel at work is to have the right amount of confidence. However, let us further discuss the ways that you can excel at work and how you can improve your confidence in the next few sections of this book.

Section 1: Boosting Your Confidence At Work

Nobody was born confident. Confidence is something that we learn as we grow up. When we were just babies, we needed somebody to take care of us. We had to depend on our parents or caretaker to feed us, bath us and even put us to sleep. But as we grow older, we learn to do little things by ourselves which will eventually make us independent people.

As we grow up, our confidence or self-esteem either goes up or down depending on different factors that can influence our self-esteem or our confidence. What are these factors?

- The environment at home. The way your parents treat you and how the people at home behave and treat each other can affect the confidence level that you have.
- School can also affect one's confidence level. Were the teachers and classmates able to provide a person room to improve his or her self-confidence?
- Media has strong influence on a person's self-esteem especially when it comes to the physical appearance.
- Feedback can affect one's confidence too. Somebody who gets too much negative feedback will start feeling bad about himself and confidence level gradually goes down.
- The consequences of our actions can also affect our confidence.
- Another important thing that can affect our confidence is how we handle any situation whether good or bad.

Even when you are at work, you still need to be confident because the confidence level that you have will affect how well you do your job. But do you ever ask yourself if you are confident enough? If you are not quite sure about this, check the list below and see if you have any of the signs.

- When you do something, you have the need to explain your actions to others. A person who has enough confidence in his abilities will not feel the need to do so. Even people who are successful but lacks self confidence will still feel the need to explain why they made certain decisions.

- Constantly complaining about others and blaming them for whatever you are complaining about is another sign of low or lack of self-confidence. You avoid taking responsibility by blaming it on others.

- When somebody criticizes you do you make excuses? If so, then you lack self-confidence. Making excuses is one of the things people do to avoid thinking about themselves as useless.

- People who lack self-confidence are always defensive and feel the need to keep shutting out other people. There defensiveness can also be seen in their body language.

- Needing the frequent approval of others is another sign of low self-confidence. When you don't get the validation that you need, you start to get frustrated and it decreases your self-confidence even further.

- Some people do not enjoy the success they have earned because they lack self-confidence. They do not think that it was their competence that got them the success but rather they think they were just lucky.

- Even though you are in a situation that you no longer find satisfactory, you choose to stay in the same situation because you of the fear that they have about change.

- You exude an air of negativity. You do not think that you have the right skills to do anything and you take it out on the people around you.

- A person who lacks confidence feel that they need to be perfect and if they are not meeting the expectations that they have set for themselves, they feel ashamed about it.

Think about what you just read for a few minutes and reflect. Do you have any of the signs you just read about?

If your answer is yes, then don't worry because we always have tips for your to help you increase your self-confidence at work. Continue reading to know what these habits are and make sure you do your best to put these habits into daily use.

- Trumpeting your achievement at work

When you tell people about any success that you have, you are not necessarily being boastful about it. It all depends on how you say it. If you do achieve any form of success in your work, you are allowed to tell others about it. How does this help improve your self-confidence? You are acknowledging the contribution that you have made for the company. You are allowing yourself to enjoy the reward of being hardworking and diligent by savoring the success that were a result of your actions.

- Be confident about finishing a task.

So one of your peers just told you to do something, what should you do? Should you tell them you cannot do it? Should you tell them that you will see what you can do about it? Nope. The answer should neither be those two options. Instead, tell them with all the confidence that you can muster that you are going to finish the task that they are assigning to you.

When you say your intention out loud, which is to finish a certain task, you start building your confidence in what you can do. Saying it out loud, with your workmates knowing about it, means you are making yourself accountable for the outcome of the task. But of course you should not just leave it at that, saying you will finish the task. You need to follow through with what you said. Saying you will finish a task is a good confidence booster but not finishing the task is one good way to kill your confidence.

Look at bullying as a change motivator.

Have you been bullied when you were still in school? It was a bad experience wasn't it? You just could not wait to graduate from school to get rid of the bullying. But unfortunately, bullying does not only happen in schools. They happen everywhere and they happen even at work where there are grown ups.

Bullying or personal attacks can happen to anybody at work. When you are slowly climbing up the corporate ladder, somebody is going to try to take you down. Or when somebody just wants to be close to the boss, that person would do anything to make himself look good and make others look bad, including yourself. But how should you react to these personal attacks?

Do not allow yourself to be a victim of these personal attacks. It may be hard to do it but you should learn to let go of any anger or resentment against the attacker. Learn to look at these attacks as a way to improve yourself and to mature. What can you do about yourself to prevent yourself from getting anymore of these attacks?

So if somebody tells you that you do not have any idea or opinion on a subject matter because you keep quiet all the time, then take this as an opportunity to learn how to speak your thoughts.

- Speaking Your Mind

If you're at a meeting where everyone is expected to contribute something, don't just sit there and watch as the others exchange ideas. But this does not mean that you should say everything that is on your mind and not having any filters.

The things you say should always be appropriate or relevant to the discussion. If your boss or peers ask you for your opinion on a particular client, keep your answer related to that and don't veer off. A person who lacks confidence does not have guts to say what is on his mind. This can lead to regrets. When you share your thoughts about something, you see how the others react to it. This builds your confidence because you will be able to adjust accordingly as well.

- Training Yourself

Many of us lack confidence because we feel like we do not have enough skills to do our job. Some of us think that we are not well equipped to do the task at hand. But luckily, this is a problem that can be easily resolved as long as you are dedicated to the solution. So what should you do? Enroll yourself in short courses that will give you better knowledge in relation to your work.

There are many courses both online and offline. All you need to do is to find the right one for you. If you do not have the money or the time to personally attend a class, then you can always take up online courses. There are many online references that you can check out. And these are courses that you can do on your own, whenever it is convenient for you.

When you supplement your current knowledge with these additional courses, you are taking away that feeling of being inadequate.

Bouncing Criticisms

Every now and then, we encounter criticisms that are simply too much for us to handle and it drains our energy just like that. You have worked so hard to keep your confidence level at a certain level. Should you allow a single criticism to destroy the fruit of your hard work? Definitely not. So what should you do?

Instead of letting yourself think about the criticism that zapped your self-confidence, choose to ignore it. What you should do instead is to remind yourself of the other good things that you have, your skills and your abilities. One below-the-belt criticism should not overshadow the many good things about you.

So how does rejecting this kind of criticism work? When you think so much about a negative feedback, you are slowly draining yourself of whatever confidence you have.

Thus rejecting the criticism prevents that from happening.
- Smile More Often

If you have not noticed, the confident people have a tendency to smile more often instead of sulking or keeping their heads down when they walk around the office. Yes, smiling more often is not something that can happen with just a snap of your finger. It is something that you need to work on.

When you are in the office, smile and greet your coworkers. Ask them how their day is going. You'll be surprised to see how much better your outlook will be. This change in attitude and outlook is so contagious that it will also be visible in your level of confidence.

Keep That Bounce In Your Step

Yes, this actually works. How you carry yourself affects how you feel about yourself. Your body language will reflect whatever confidence you have. When you walk around the office, keep your head up. Having a little more energy with every step that you take is one good way to boost your confidence.

- Surround Yourself With The Right People

You can also boost your self-confidence with help from other people. Instead of being in the company of people who have nothing but criticisms for you, why don't you surround yourself with people who can actually see the good side of you? Having people around you that are able to point out what you've done right is definitely a good way to boost your confidence. And when the time comes that you feel a little low, these same people can also help encourage you to see the good that they see.

If you are not sure about a presentation you are about to give in the next meeting, your supportive friends can always help you out. Give them a mock presentation. They will be able to provide you some helpful insights so that you'll be more confident during your presentation.

Take the time to review the people you have surrounded yourself with. If you notice that most of them are giving you criticisms that are no constructive in any way, then maybe it is time to start searching for new people to hang out with.

○ Acceptance

You are going to make mistakes every now and then. Learning to accept the fact that we are imperfect will help you cope better when problems arise. You won't be too hard on yourself.

Boosting your confidence at work or even at home is not going to happen overnight. You need to have patience and dedication.

Section 2: How To Excel At Work

Sometimes we wonder why others are getting promoted while we are still in the same position that we were in when we started this job? Where did you go wrong? Is there anything that you can do to improve yourself? Or how about starting a new job? What should you be doing to excel at work?

Regardless of your reason for wanting to excel at work, there are many things that you can do to make sure that you are providing an excellent quality of service at work. It is not just about being good at what you do. Excelling at work involves many other things. Here are some excellent tips that you can try to do in order to excel at work.

- Keep Eyes On The Road

If you are just starting a new job, do not think about the promotions as a justification of all your hard work or the only thing that you should be aiming for when you work. Let us take a look at this example: you want to lose weight. Many of us prefer to look at the number of kilograms that we lose over a period of time and many of us tend to ignore the bigger picture. What's this bigger picture?

When we lose weight, we have to eat healthy and have a healthy lifestyle. This results into a healthier you that is less at risk of getting diseases. Yes, for people that aim to lose weight, the number of kilos/pounds shed is important but what's more important is the benefits that you get from the weight that you lost.

That's what you should focus on. So going back to the work situation, do not focus all your attention on getting that promotion. Instead focus on how competent you are, your behavior towards you work and your colleagues, and your expectations. When you focus on this instead of the promotion itself, you are going to learn a lot more in the long run and you'll be surprised to know that you got the promotion much faster than you would have if you only focused on the promotion itself.

Do A Great Job

There are people who do their job and there are those who do their job well. There is a clear distinction between the two. While they are the same in the sense that the job is still done, the latter group (those who do their job well) goes the extra mile. They give in extra effort.

They do not just do the job required from them but they make sure that they exceed what is expected from them. If you really want to stand out from the rest, you need to make sure that you step up your game. Do not just be that person who makes coffee but make someone who makes delicious coffee.

○ Work Really Hard

Do not expect to excel when you just show up at work and not really get any work done. We no longer live in a time where employees showing up for work is already enough. When you are at work, you need to work.

You cannot just sit around in your office, gazing at your screen or going out every now and then to attend to personal issues. When you are working, you need to make sure that you are at work on time and you stay there until office hours are over. Do not be surprised either when you need to extend your office hours to finish any task that you have left for the day.

When you are at work, you need to make sure that you keep yourself busy with things that are relevant to your work. Answer email and phone inquiries, finish a file you've been asked to do, read and sign documents and whatever else is needed from you by your employers.

◦ Be A Professional

Yes, life is boring without any sense of humor or being so serious all the time. But you need to remember that everything has a right place and your workplace is not the right time to clown around, unless you happen to be a clown.

But seriously, when you are at work, you are expected to be taking your job seriously and not be fooling around with your colleagues. Regardless of the kind of job you have, your employer expects you to be focused. You need to act like a professional. You need to treat your colleagues, clients and work matters as professionally as you can. If you have any problems at home, do not take them with you when you go to work.

Lashing out on your workmates because you had an argument with your spouse earlier is not how a professional would act. It is not professionalism either when you show up at work an hour late, unless you have a very valid reason for doing so. Professionalism also includes being dressed appropriately for your work. If you are a CEO, you are expected to look the part. You cannot come to work just wearing your favorite pair of shorts and shirt.

◦ Have A Positive Attitude

No, you are not expected to be over-the-moon cheerful otherwise no one will take you seriously. What you should have instead is a a go-get-it attitude and we-can-do-this attitude. If you had a co-worker that complained all the time or who kept saying you cannot do this because of a million reasons, would you like to continue working with that person? You probably wouldn't.

One's attitude is contagious and having a negative attitude can also bring down your co-workers outlook too. And besides, it is simply hard to work with somebody who has too much negativity around him because it is annoying.

◦ Take Initiative

Aside from being very good at your job, you should also learn to take initiatives. Do not just be satisfied with what you have now and how your department is working or organized. If you see ways to further improve how your department works, take the initiative.

Make suggestions to the right people or take the first step in order for that change to happen. If you can see any other way that can help you do your job better, do not be afraid to do so. Pushing the limits in order to be a better employee with a department that works better is a wonderful way to exceed. However, you need to realize as well that having the initiative to initiate changes or improve things is not the same as knowing it all so do not confuse one for the other.

◦ Have Right Conversations

If you want to have a clear picture of what you should be doing in order to go to the next level, the best way to do it is to directly talk to your boss about it. Do it in a tactful manner though. You could ask him things like what is expected from you in the next few months and what you should be doing in order to move up to the next level.

◦ Postpone The Entitlement

You might think that you already deserve a promotion and so you demand this from your boss. However, you need to realize that many people consider themselves ready for a promotion even before they actually are.

Promotions are not just based on your work performance. You need to realize that there are other factors to be considered when promoting an employee. First, is there any available position to promote anyone to?

Do they have the right leadership skills? How well does they mingle with coworkers? How does they cope with stressful situations? These are just some of the considerations that an employer has to make prior to making any promotions. And you need to remember that you are not the only person that is being considered for the promotion too.

It may not hurt if you talk to the boss about it but still, you need to remember to do it tactfully without demanding that you have to be promoted because of this and that. That might completely turn off your boss and they might never ever consider to promote you ever again.

◦ Be A Team Player

Many of the companies today have employees working in teams. If you want to be able to excel as a whole in your workplace, it is very important that you are a great team player. What does being a great team player include? You need to be able to communicate well with your teammates and you need to be able to handle well both the success and failure of the team. It is important that you review important issues regarding the team and your role in the team.

If you want to get a better insight on how well you are able to work with your teammates, the best way to do this is to ask your teammates. Ask them to give you honest feedback. From their feedback, you will be able to determine the areas that you need to work on in order for you to be a better team player.

◦ Get To Know Your Boss

This does not really mean that you have to be best buds with your boss. But rather, you need to have a better understanding of how your boss thinks, how they act, what they prefer, their expectations and what they do not like. When you know these things about your boss, it is easier to meet their expectations and demands from you. You know what makes them tick and you know the things that you should do if you want to remain on their good side.

◦ Understand Your Employer

Aside from getting to know your superior, you also need to have a better understanding of the company that employed you. It is common to find employees that have been working in the same company for years but they have no clear understanding of the mission, objectives and strategies of their employer. Knowing these details will also help you determine the right course of action in order to do your role in the company properly and accordingly.

◦ Gracefully Accept Criticisms

While there are criticisms that you should just completely shake off, there are criticisms too that you must learn to handle. When the criticisms are about how you are handling your job, you need to learn to accept it. It can be very hard but if you do it often enough, it will become easier. Instead of starting grownup tantrums, sit down and listen to what your boss has to say.

Think carefully about it and reflect on the things that you could do in order to improve your performance at work. You must also remember that the bosses are giving you these criticisms in order for you to do your job better. And you know what happens when you do your job better. You are going to excel in your work. That's what we all want, isn't it?

° Grab Opportunities

It is easy to get bored when you do the same thing over and over again. We stop being excellent in our job and the workplace suddenly becomes more dull. But you can prevent this from happening. If your employer gives you opportunities to acquire new skills or to broaden your knowledge, do not be afraid to take these opportunities. These opportunities of learning is a great way to excel at work.

° Be a solution-provider

Don't you just hate it when your co-workers point out a string of problems without really providing any solution? Do not just stop at pointing out what the problem is. If you really want to excel, you need to be part of the solution as well. If you see any problems with the job, the team, the product or service or even the company, point it out.

At the same time, come up with ideas that can help resolve these solutions. Employers like to have employees that are able to come up with solutions to daily problems in the workplace and it is one way for you to shine above the rest.

Conclusion

Most people who are working at a company are aiming to be an excellent employee. Some want to excel at work because they want to impress the boss and be promoted to higher positions. However, you should note that doing an excellent job in the workplace is also a good way for you to feel satisfied about yourself overall. Excelling in your job will give you great confidence and having a good confidence level is also necessary if you were to excel in your job. These are two things that go hand in hand.

Being confident is especially necessary for those who are just starting out in a new job. If you are too shy to speak up and ask questions about how things are done, you are likely to stumble and grope your way around the workplace blindly. While there is nothing wrong with trying to figure things out on your own, there are some things that are best done with help from others. It is easier to excel when you are confident about what you should be doing.

You can surely excel at work and boost your confidence if you follow the tips that we have listed in the previous sections. Remember that these things take time before they can be a habit so do not expect changes to happen overnight. You have to work hard for these changes to happen and build your confidence over time.

www.ingramcontent.com/pod-product-compliance
Lightning Source LLC
Chambersburg PA
CBHW071811020426
42331CB00008B/2461